SLOTH

COLORING BOOK

This book belongs to:

____

WHY
drink
COFFEE
when
YOU CAN
nap

Naps
are
UNDERRATED

REST NOW
WORK LATER

JUST DO IT!
(WHEN YOU CAN)

HURRY UP
and
REST!

OH
WAS THAT
DUE TODAY?

TOO TIRED
TO LISTEN NOW

SORRY
IT'S
BREAK
TIME

I COULD HURRY
BUT WHY

LAZY?
YOU MEAN RESERVING MY ENERGY?

SOME HUMANS DO DRUGS.
I DO NAPS

SLOTH'S FAVORITE DANCE?
SLOW DANCE!

FROM 1 TO SLOTH
HOW LAZY ARE YOU?

IS 'SLOTH' A CAREER OPTION?
TO DO:
FIX
DEADLINES

TOMORROW'S
A NEW DAY
TODAY I'M DOING NOTHING

I Have PH.D*
*IN Laziness

Don't worry
BE SLOTHY

A WISE SLOTH ONCE SAID:
Slow & steady wins

TAKE
A NAP
IN FACT,
TAKE TWO

SLOW
down
AND ENJOY
NAPS

I'LL get THERE...
Eventually.

SLOW DOWN BUDDY.
IT'S SLOTH
POLICE

GONNA
NEED SOME
extra PILLOWS!

NAPS
JUST TAKE
THEM

Made in the USA
Monee, IL
25 April 2020

28056331R00031